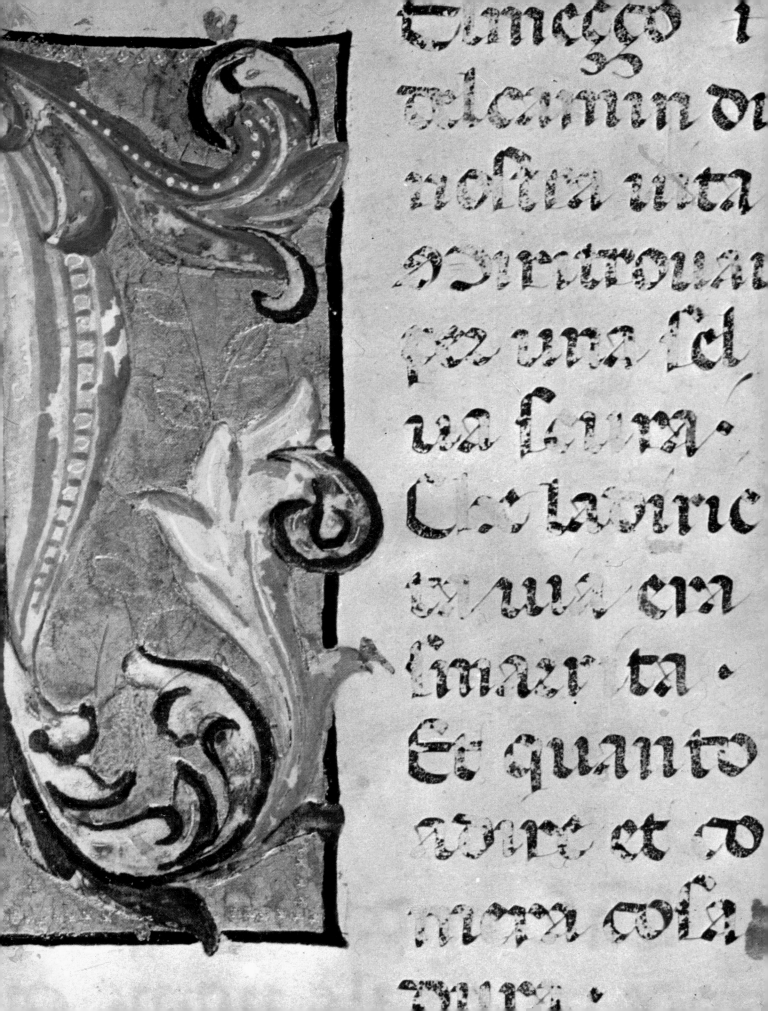

CURTIS INTERNATIONAL
PORTRAITS OF GREATNESS

General Editor
Dr. Enzo Orlandi

Text by
Maria Luisa Rizzatti

Translator
Salvator Attanasio

Published by
ARNOLDO MONDADORI EDITORE
and
THE CURTIS PUBLISHING COMPANY

THE
LIFE
&
TIMES
OF
DANTE

CURTIS BOOKS
A division of
The Curtis Publishing Company
Philadelphia • New York

GIFT

CIVITAS · FLORENTIE

LIFE
AND WORK
INTERTWINED

We can get an idea of the density and intricacy of Dante's Florence from the fresco (left) in the hall of the Commissario del Bigallo in Florence. The city had a population of about 40,000 at that time. The allegory (below) by Convenevole da Prato provides an image of the city's growing prosperity.

The life of Dante Alighieri, considered by many to be the father of Italian poetry, is inextricably bound up with his greatest work, the *Divine Comedy*. A poem in three parts, the *Inferno*, the *Purgatorio*, and the *Paradiso*, it was the first major work to be written in the vernacular, Italian, rather than in the Latin of medieval authors. Thus, it ushered in the flowering of the Romance languages which took place during the Renaissance. Yet it is probably unsurpassed by any later work written in Italian.

The basic plot of the *Comedy* is simple. The poet and narrator, wandering lost in a wood on Good Friday in 1300, meets the spirit of Virgil, the greatest of Latin poets and author of the *Aeneid*. Virgil acts as his guide through Hell and Purgatory, where they hear the stories and observe the torments of a variety of sinners. Ascending a mountain, they reach the Earthly Paradise. Here Virgil must stop because, as a product of the pre-Christian era, he is incapable of receiving Grace. But Dante finds another guide in Beatrice, based on a woman whom in real life the poet knew and loved. It is she who conducts him through Paradise, purifying him for the final revelation of God.

Nowhere in literature is there such a detailed picture of Heaven and Hell as Dante presents in the *Divine Comedy*. Its geography is explicit, the punishments and rewards of its inhabitants scrupulously based on their behavior before death. The *Inferno* is especially vivid; the poet's genius allows us to feel pity for many of the tormented souls, although it is clear that their own actions have brought them through the gates of Hell, sternly inscribed: "All hope abandon, ye who enter here." The poem is on one level an allegory, describing Dante's passage from sin and error, through earthly knowledge as represented by Virgil, to a state of grace. At the same time, it is a political and social history of the Italy in which Dante lived, especially of the beloved Florence which had banished him. Many of the personages who appear were Dante's contemporaries; his own friends and enemies were included, along with great figures from the historical and legendary past.

The poetry of the *Divine Comedy* is immortal. Literary document though it is, it has never been relegated to the dusty shelves of scholarship. Not only has everyone who knows Italian read it in the original, but much of its language has been incorporated into everyday speech. The ordinary Italian, regardless of rank or education, knows and loves its characters like members of his own family. It is no wonder that we tend to forget which incidents belong to Dante's real life and which to his poetic journey, when his countrymen over 600 years later are still living with the fruits of his imagination. Thus the *Comedy* is an unequaled popular phenomenon, as well as a brilliant work of art.

A CROWDED, QUARRELSOME FLORENCE

Dante's Florence was a typical Italian city of the late Middle Ages—small, grim, unadorned. After the year 1000, it had begun to spread beyond the old perimeter of the Roman encampment to which it owed its origin. The growth continued beyond the second circle of walls, and in 1284, when Dante was 19, the *Signoria*, or governing council, considered the construction of a third wall, to include boroughs strewn with vineyards, orchards and new convents. Within the old walls the city, with its narrow, malodorous streets in which hens scratched among the garbage and pigs wallowed in the mire, grew more and more crowded.

The Florentines, packed closely together, were cramped and quarrelsome. The city was dark even in the daytime, because the shadows of the fortress-like houses fell across the streets.

Demolition was a favorite sport with the Florentines. As soon as the heads of a faction were proscribed, their adversaries dismantled their houses. In 1260, five years before Dante's birth, the Guelph faction saw their houses torn down; in 1266 the Ghibelline homes were destroyed. When Dante was one year old, the blows of pickaxes hacking down the once-proud walls of the residence of the Ubertis, the heads of a defeated faction, could be heard from the spot where he played. The towers, which once had risen like a forest of stone, were now almost all reduced to sinister-looking stumps. The citizens of Florence were constantly suspended between the fear of ambush and the sound of the alarm.

When the Florentine bourgeoisie was not thinking about waging war, it was thinking about making money. They were a practical people. Even the palaces of the rich were strictly functional. The first floors were used to store merchandise; the towers and bastions were for defense, not decoration. Arrow-slits were everywhere. The churches were small, modest. Only one of them shone like a jewel on a verdant hilltop: San Miniato al Monte. The most notable monument within the city's walls was the Baptistery, Dante's "bel San Giovanni." It was still in a rough, unfinished state. The covering was to begin in 1294, and the memory of the white-green marble façade was to haunt the dreams of the poet in exile with an obsessive sweetness. Florence, at once loved and hated, was the strongest earthly bond that Dante knew, a counterpoise to his wholly spiritual devotion to Beatrice. He was to remain faithful to only two loves: the woman and the city of his youth.

Two portraits of Dante have been handed down to us: One as a youth, one as a grown man. The latter (on the adjoining page) has given us the traditional idea of what he looked like. It is in Codex 1040, preserved in the Riccardiana Library in Florence.

Left: The oldest part of the Palazzo del Podestà, also called the Bargello, whose construction was begun around 1254. It was the residence of the podestà *(mayor) Cante de' Gabrielli da Gubbio, who pronounced the first sentence against Dante as a "thief and swindler" in January, 1302. Above: Two panels from Giotto's bell tower. The artist was a friend of Dante.*

Here are some of the places linked to Dante's youth. Below: The cloister of Santa Maria Novella, which was built after Dante's time but in the same convent where he went to study philosophy. Below: The polyhedron structure of the Baptistery of San Giovanni, where Dante was baptized in 1266 and where, when he was on the verge of death, he hoped to be crowned with the poet's laurel.

Right: The medieval palace of the Guelph party, which was restored in the 19th century. Below: The Gate of the Cross (Porta alla Croce), built toward the end of the 13th century, formed part of the third circle of the city's walls which enclosed Florence until the 19th century. It was demolished when Florence was the capital of Italy. The gates were preserved.

Left: The building of the woolen workers, one of the most important guilds of medieval Florence. The members of this guild contributed to the construction of Santa Maria del Fiore. Below: The cloisters of the Franciscan basilica of Santa Croce, whose construction began in Dante's time. The poet continued his philosophical studies here.

Below: The extraordinarily beautiful façade of San Miniato al Monte, which was a familiar sight to Dante. It was the most important monastic church built outside the city walls. Bottom: The courtyard of the building of the Captain of the People (Capitano del Popolo), later called the Bargello. The oldest part was built during the poet's youth.

DANTE'S EARLY LIFE

No undeniably authentic portrait of Dante exists today, nor a line written by his own hand. His house was destroyed to its foundations; what is now called "Dante's house" is a 19th-century reconstruction. Even his remains were subject to thefts, additions, and reconstitutions. Few documents mention him, even ambiguously. To know what Dante was really like, we must refer to the *Divine Comedy*.

The exact day of Dante's birth in May, 1265, is unknown. He came from an aristocratic family which could be traced back to the Crusades. His father and mother both died before Dante reached adolescence. At his father's death, Dante and three step-brothers found themselves in very modest financial circumstances. The family, like the whole feudal nobility, was already losing ground to the new communal bourgeoisie.

On February 9, 1277, according to a sworn notary document of the time, Dante Alighieri and Gemma Donati were married. The bridegroom was not yet 12, the bride perhaps 10. Gemma belonged to one of the most prominent families in Florence, and brought her husband a respectable dowry. In those days, marriage was an alliance between two families, arranged by their elder members. The union would be consummated when the couple grew up.

Meanwhile, the bridegroom was attending school. After completing primary school, he passed on to the Trivium and the Quadrivium, liberal arts courses which offered Latin, geometry, arithmetic, astronomy (actually astrology) and music, to which he was to be passionately attached all his life. He also learned to write verse, an art at which all the intellectuals of Florence tried their hand.

Left: The Castagna tower, which was the first seat of the Priors of the Arts in Dante's time. Center: The tiny church of S. Martino del Vescovo, a 15th-century construction, but linked by its name and partially by its location with the ancient parish of the Alighieri family. Right: A part of the arbitrary reconstruction which was made at the beginning of the 19th century, called "Dante's house."

THE WANING
MIDDLE AGES

Despite civic discords, Florence fundamentally was a prosperous city. There was plenty of money around, and people began to discover the sweetness of life. Even rich men's houses were bare according to medieval practice, but tapestries for the walls and luxurious bedspreads were coming into fashion. Meals, one served at midmorning, the other just before nightfall, consisted of abundant meat, spices and wine; the Tuscans were adept huntsmen, so game was never lacking. Forks and napkins were unknown, but at the banquets a storyteller or buffoon was provided to entertain the guests. On solemn occasions there were musicians instead. Music was one of the liberal arts of the Trivium and Quadrivium, so every cultured person was expected to know at least the fundamentals of the art. Dante had a very acute sensitivity to music. One of his songs, *Love That in My Mind Discourseth to Me*, was set to music by Casella. In the *Divine Comedy*, Dante meets him on the landing-place of Purgatory, and beseeches him to show him his song again. The sporting contests of the time, foot or horse races, are also recalled in the *Comedy*. Weddings, baptisms, religious feasts, the arrivals and departures of illustrious personages, even funeral cortèges, were transformed into convivial social occasions, sometimes also into bloody scrimmages. The vitality of a people too long repressed in the Middle Ages now surged to the surface, threatening an explosion at any moment.

The virtues and vices of humanity, and the liberal arts, are the themes of these miniatures by Nicoló da Bologna, taken from a 14th-century Codex in the Ambrosiana Library in Milan. The "arts" were important guild organizations which in Florence were divided into the majors and the minors. The latter included manual workers, who had the right to organize.

13

THE NEW BREED

In Florence in the second half of the 13th century,
the aristocracy of blood made way for the aristocracy
of money. Although theoretically subject to the authority of the German emperor, the city was in fact a free
republic, dominated by the bourgeois element. The
poetry of the New Style, of which Dante was the
standard-bearer, denied the values of the Middle Ages.
The "magnates by accident" succeeded the "magnates
by nature," the scions of the old landed aristocracy.
The new breed of magnates were the big bankers who
financed the sovereigns of Europe, the merchants who
invaded public squares in Italy and abroad with woolen
cloth, silks and furs. Abroad they were generally called
"Lombards," but in reality they were mainly from the
district of Tuscany, of which Florence was a part. In a
time notorious for its bad roads and wretched trans-
portation, it was routine for these enterprising merchants to buy raw cloth in England or Flanders, process
it in Florence and distribute it all over Europe. They
were away from home for long months at a time, send-
ing back news from Antwerp, London and the Orient.
The youthful and progressive spirit of the new mer-
chant class was gathering strength.

*During the early Middle Ages
trade was primarily concentrated
in the great traditional fairs.
In the 13th century the fairs
began to wane, while markets
sprang up vigorously, becoming the
hub of urban activity. The picture
on the adjoining page gives us
an idea of the intense activity
and movement of the Florentine
market. It is taken from the
Codex known as "il Biadaiolo"
in the Laurentian Library
in Florence.*

14

THE COLOR
OF PEARL

Dante was only nine years old when he fell in love with Beatrice, the woman who became his inspiration and symbol. We don't know whether she was a blonde or a brunette. The poet is rarely concerned with her looks: in the *Vita Nuova* (*New Life*), he describes her complexion as "the color of pearl." Her warm and transparent pallor fascinated Dante: in the *Paradise* we find the image of a feminine forehead so white that he can barely distinguish a pearl in the center of a golden headband, which fashionable ladies wore at that time. Dante himself was so dark-skinned that, according to his early biographers, people on the streets, seeing him, would whisper that his dark complexion came from his subterranean journey among the flames of hell. In the *Purgatorio*, Beatrice's eyes are called emeralds. Some commentators contend that the image alludes to brightness without necessarily specifying a color. But on the other hand, Dante was never at a loss for a rhyme, and he was too knowledgeable about stones to cite emeralds by chance. It is reasonable to suppose that Beatrice's eyes were truly green.

Beatrice's brief earthly life is as obscure as her appearance. According to the *Vita Nuova*, the two met at the age of nine. Beatrice was dressed in red, "a most noble sanguine color." They saw each other again at the age of 18, and this time Beatrice was dressed in white. Beatrice was almost certainly the daughter of Folco Portinari, an eminent citizen of Florence and founder of the hospital of S. Maria Nuova. If so, the infrequency of their meetings is a poetic invention: the Portinaris lived only a few steps away from Dante's house and, no matter how segregated the life led by young girls in the 13th century, there certainly could have been no lack of opportunities for seeing one another. Nevertheless, a marriage was out of the question. Dante was betrothed to Gemma Donati; Beatrice eventually married Simone de' Bardi and died at the age of 25 in 1290. The love between them was wholly spiritual. Death had no dominion over such a bond. After her death Dante realized that she was more alive than ever. When he sees her again on Mount Purgatory, she is not a dead girl, but a woman who speaks with authority; she reproaches him vigorously, and then becomes maternal, radiant and comforting.

Among the painters of the 19th century who were dedicated to glorifying Beatrice, a prominent place indubitably is occupied by Dante Gabriel Rossetti. The son of an Italian exile, this English artist was the standard-bearer of the Pre-Raphaelite movement, which flourished in England toward the end of the 19th century, and drew its inspiration from the earliest Italian art. Besides a Beata Beatrix *in which he portrayed the features of his wife, Lizzie, D. G. Rossetti painted* The Greeting of Beatrice *(left), inspired by the* Vita Nuova, *which he translated into English. Above: Another of the many 19th-century representations of Beatrice.*

"THE BRAZEN-FACED WOMEN OF FLORENCE"

The passion for fancy dress was one of the characteristics of the time. In vain did oldtimers like Dante's great-great-grandfather Cacciaguida, in the *Comedy*, deplore the passing of the age when even the most prominent citizens were content with simple clothes and rough leather belts with buckles made of bone. Now they wanted silks, brocades and furs: the belts were adorned with precious stones. The "brazen-faced women of Florence," with their extremely low-necked gowns, aroused Dante's indignation. For the Florentine man, dress was a sign of his official position and his economic status. For the Florentine woman, it was the source of her charm. High heels became fashionable in the late Middle Ages. The moralists waxed indignant over the pretexts they found to display an elegant shoe or an adorned ankle. From the pulpits the clergy raged against certain fashions, but even at that time women somehow found a way to get around such obstacles. Thus when it was decided that to cover her head was a sign of modesty in woman, fashion turned to veils of thin muslin and silk woven with gold which drew even more glances from admiring males than had their uncovered tresses. Blond hair was also fashionable; those who were not so favored by nature dyed their own hair, using a so-called "blonding hat." It was a curious headgear without a crown and provided with a very large brim on which the locks of hair were arranged in an aureole. Thus arrayed, the ladies sat for hours on the belvederes or, as time went on, even on their ancestral turrets. If a sunstroke did not interrupt the treatment, the result was certain. The mania for jewelry was general among the wealthy classes; it afflicted men as well as women. Bracelets were in vogue, rings for every finger, and even diadems. Even Dante succumbed to the enthusiasm for gems. But as a man of culture he tends to neglect the ornamental or financial value of jewels in order to glorify their hidden virtues (which the stars influence) and their rich symbolism. Images of precious stones shine forth from the moment he arrives at the threshold of Purgatory and blaze with a dazzling light in Paradise.

On this page and at the side: Examples of the feminine elegance of Dante's time, painted by his friend, Giotto, in the frescoes of the Paduan chapel of the Scrovegni. The scenes are of religious inspiration—the wedding at Cana, the encounter at the Golden Gate, the entry into Jerusalem—but the costumes and hair styles are of Dante's time. The refinement of the feminine fashions strikes us as being relatively modern, a change from the forced austerity of the Middle Ages. Complicated coiffures, with ribbons and skullcaps, became a mania among the ladies.

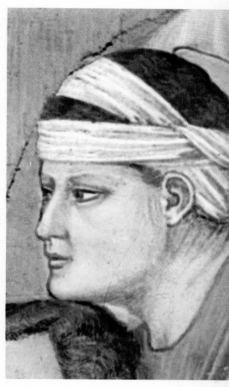

These are the costly garments
inveighed against by Dante's
ancestor, Cacciaguida, who
deplores the passing of the good
old days of simple and sober tastes.
The shade of Forese Donati,
encountered in Purgatory, also
castigates the "brazen-faced
women of Florence." Preachers,
he says, will be forced to prohibit
the immodesty of such fashions
from the pulpit. In reality Dante
was very sensitive to feminine
elegance, to which he also
attributed symbolic meaning.
Thus in the Vita Nuova and in
the Comedy, Beatrice appears
in a red gown, with a green
mantle and a white veil.

This painting by Giorgio Vasari, now at Oxford's Oriel College, is called The Poets of Florence. *Vasari, a 16th-century painter, was a native of Arezzo and the first historian of Italian art; he portrayed Dante in the center of his composition* (right) together with Petrarch and Boccaccio. Alongside this trio of great poets are the portraits of Cino da Pistoia (left) and Guido Cavalcanti (right), two of Dante's greatest contemporaries and intimate friends. The sixth poet is Guittone d'Arezzo.

FRIENDSHIPS— GOOD AND BAD

Two friends of Dante's youth symbolize two conflicting aspects of his personality: they are Forese Donati and Guido Cavalcanti, folly and wisdom, the flesh and the spirit. Forese, whose real name was Bicci, was the friend of the madcap years. He was a cousin of Dante on his wife's side, and belonged to the most prominent branch of the Donatis, whom the common people had given the eloquent nickname of *Malefami*, or the Disreputables. Companions in revelry, Dante and Forese exchanged malicious gibes in six ferocious sonnets. In them Dante reproaches Forese for his neglect of his wife, Nella, and cites the aspersions current about his origins; Forese responds with an allusion to the suspicion that Dante's father, Alighiero, was a usurer, and declares that without his step-brothers, Dante would have been lodged in the poorhouse a long time ago. His verses of this period resound with the coarse laughter and vulgar taunts of the tavern.

Guido Cavalcanti, 10 years Dante's senior and his predecessor in the school of the New Style, was the antithesis of Forese Donati. Aristocratic and proud, he was a lover of solitude who held vulgar pleasures in contempt. In a sonnet that begins: "I come to you by day an infinite number of times, and find you thinking thoughts too base," he begs Dante to give up his profligate way of life.

Other friends of the New Style circle were Lapo Gianni, the notary-poet, and Cino Sigisbuldi da Pistoia, the "amorous Messer Cino." Their carefree existence was not to last. Forese died in 1296, Guido four years later; Cino and Dante were to eat the bitter bread of exile. It was probably a presentiment of these disasters that led Dante to formulate one of his most moving poetic fantasies, in a famous youthful sonnet: in it he expresses the wish to embark on a vessel with the two friends who are closest to his heart, with their ladies and his, and glide along a placid sea without ever again touching the cruel shores of reality.

FACTIONS
AND
FEUDS

Italy in general and Tuscany in particular bred political factions. Two large political parties, the Guelphs and the Ghibellines, warred constantly in the 12th and 13th centuries. They were, respectively, partisans of the royal house of Bavaria and the royal house of Swabia, competing for control of the old Holy Roman Empire. In Florence, the old feudal nobility sided with the Ghibellines, while the Guelphs were the party of the communal bourgeoisie. The nobles saw in the German emperor the source of their power, and the bourgeoisie tried to form an alliance with the church hierarchies. These basic motivations soon got mixed up with ancient personal and family grudges and partisan struggles which had absolutely nothing to do with the Church or the Empire. In Tuscany, Pisa, Siena and Arezzo were Ghibelline, whereas Lucca and Florence were usually Guelph. All murders and quarrels could be justified by this international feud. Compatriots and coreligionists hated each other in its name: more than 4,000 Guelphs of Florence were exterminated by the Sienese and Ghibelline exiles in a single day at the battle of Montaperti, after bloody hand-to-hand combat. When Dante, through Farinata in the *Comedy*, speaks of the great slaughter which "dyed the Arbia red," he is using an all too literal image.

The painting by Amos Cassioli recalls an episode of the struggles between Guelphs and Ghibellines. Provenzano Salvani, head of the pro-imperial faction in Siena, begs publicly for money with which to ransom his friend Mino de' Mini, a prisoner of Charles d'Anjou. Dante cites this voluntary humiliation with respect in the Purgatorio.

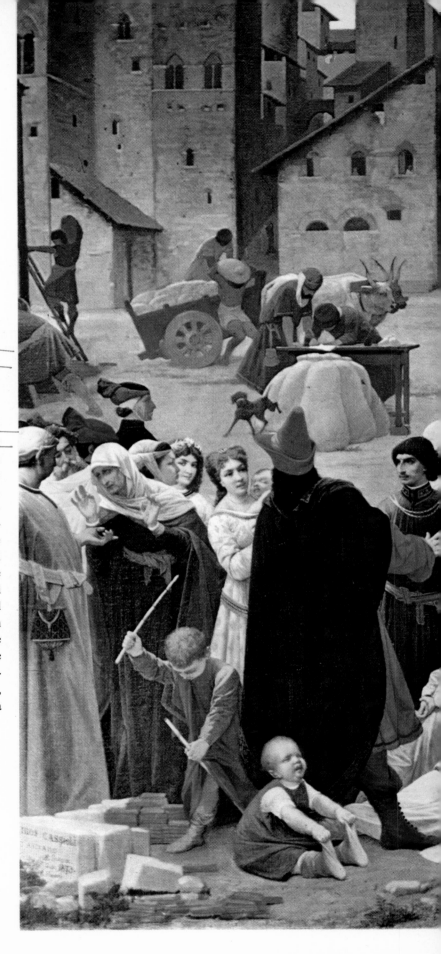

MILITARY ADVENTURES

The summer of 1289 saw Dante's debut as a soldier. He took part in the battle of Campaldino against the Ghibellines of Arezzo, and in the siege and surrender of the fortress of Caprona which was occupied by the Pisan militia. The battle with the Aretines took place on June 11, a sultry day which ended with a storm of apocalyptic violence, recalled in Canto V of the *Purgatorio*. Dante fought as a "jouster" (*feditore*) in the front ranks of the cavalry, an ancient privilege granted to noblemen. At Caprona Dante was witness to the panic fear that gripped the enemy. Besieged by the Guelph forces of Lucca and Florence, the Ghibelline foot soldiers of Pisa were forced to surrender and leave the castle, unarmed, running the gauntlet between two wings of the enemy. In the *Inferno*, Dante recalls their terror in order to describe his state of mind among the demons.

The battle of Campaldino as portrayed in an ancient miniature. The battle between the Guelph militia of Florence and the Ghibellines of Arezzo, led by Buonconte of Montefeltro and by the bishop of the city, Guglielmino degli Ubaldini, took place on June 11, 1289. Dante, who was then 24, fought on horseback as a feditore. *The Florentine troops entered Aretine territory by crossing the pass at Consuma. The outcome of the battle remained uncertain for a long time; then Corso Donati, a brother of Forese, succeeded with a bold maneuver in sowing panic in the enemy camp. Both leaders of the Aretines fell in the bloody battle.*

Below, left: The tower and remains of the fortress of Caprona, whose siege and surrender Dante witnessed in August, 1289. To the side and below: Interiors of the fortress of Poppi in Casentino, which belonged to the Counts Guidi, proud Ghibellines. The Aretine leaders followed the movements of their adversaries from the dominant position of this rock.

Below: The plain of Campaldino, seen from the fortress of Poppi. The day of the battle ended with a violent storm. Dante recalls it in Canto V of the Purgatorio *where, meeting the redeemed soul of the enemy leader, Buonconte of Montefeltro, he makes him narrate the circumstances of his death and repentance "in extremis."*

POLITICAL ADVANCE
AND SOCIAL PRETENSIONS

The second half of the 13th century witnessed the triumph of the capitalistic bourgeoisie in the commune of Florence. The great Guelph families, who had been exiled in 1260 after the defeat at Montaperti, made a triumphal reentry into the city six years later; the defeat and the death of King Manfred at Benevento dashed all hopes of an imperial restoration. Now the Ghibellines were forced to leave the city; they would never return. Dante's family, although noble and traditionally Guelph, had taken no part in the exile nor in the triumphant comeback: a sign that the Alighieri were now of little consequence, despite the fact that their ancestors had fought in the Crusades. Nobody bothered to include their names on the proscription lists which, while convenient, was tantamount to being removed from the Social Register.

When Dante reached the age of 17 and, a true Tuscan, began to take an interest in politics, the communal bourgeoisie had taken a significant step forward in its rise to power. In fact, from 1282 on, the Major Arts, the seven powerful guilds which dominated the city's economic life, acquired the right to participate in the government in the person of their Priors, next to the *podestà*. The latter was always a foreigner, called in from the outside as a sort of umpire to insure impartial conduct. In reality, these *podeste* were often charged with selling out to the highest bidder. Eleven years later democracy triumphed with Gianno della Bella, an "enlightened" aristocrat. His Ordinances of Justice approved in 1293, admitted to the Priorate only those who were signed-up members of the guilds. The Priorate accounted for 21 government posts between the majors, the medians and the minors. In other words, he who did not work, did not govern. To retain his political eligibility, Dante joined the Guild of Doctors and Druggists, which was most in keeping with his status as an intellectual. He became a member of the Priorate in 1300. He was now 35, an intellectual of some prestige, a politician of a certain weight, linked by marriage to a great family, and the father of four children: Giovanni, Pietro, Jacopo and Antonia, the future Sister Beatrice. The future seemed to belong to him. Nobody had an inkling of the misfortune that was to dog his steps.

On the adjoining page: A partisan act of revenge, from a Vatican Codex. The podestà of Florence, Cante de' Gabrielli da Gubbio, pronounces a death sentence by decapitation against some citizens belonging to the White party. He condemned Dante to banishment and burning at the stake in absentia in March, 1302. Below: An illustration of the Calendimaggio skirmish between the Whites and the Blacks in 1300, named for the day on which it took place, the May Day feast celebrating the coming of spring. Second from the left is Corso Donati, the recognized leader of the Black party, whom the Florentines called "the Baron." Below: the administration of justice according to the Ordinances of Giano della Bella.

In photograph (top), from left: Three
historical Florentine palaces. The first two,
in Borgo dei Santi Apostoli, belonged to the
Buondelmonti, whose name is linked with the
"blood wedding" of 1215, which was said to have
brought Florence into the Guelph-Ghibelline
struggle. The third palace, in Via San Nicolo,
belonged to the Mozzi clan. The miniature
below shows the factional struggles in Florence,
with groups of nobles facing each other
in combat on the roofs of their palaces.

ANARCHY FOR FLORENCE—
EXILE FOR DANTE

The miniature below represents a climactic moment in the struggles of Dante's time. Corso Donati entered the city on November 5, 1301, at the head of a band of soldiers, and threw open the prisons, ushering in a week of terror. Corso ruled the city as a dictator for the next seven years. He was killed in a brawl in 1308.

When Dante was selected to be a Prior, the fight was no longer between Guelphs and Ghibellines, but between the Whites and the Blacks. The upshot, however, was the same: Florence was more than ever a "divided city" torn by factional strife and discord. The expulsion of the Ghibellines in 1266 produced only an illusory truce. Soon the Guelph party itself was divided into two opposing factions. The bourgeois Whites were merchants, bankers and manufacturers—the "fat people" in the slang of the time; the Blacks represented what was left of the ancient feudal aristocacy, and the proletariat, which allied itself with the nobles out of hatred of the bourgeoisie. It was in the year 1300 that the long-smoldering hostility between the two parties broke out in bloody and clamorous acts of violence. It was also the year of Dante's priorship. He was in office only two months, from June 15 to August 14. The Blacks and the Whites had already come to blows on the piazza of S. Trinità during the *Calendimaggio*, the May Day celebration of the advent of spring. Blood was shed again on June 23, on the eve of the Feast of St. John, as the Consuls of the Arts, all Blacks, were going to church to make the usual votive offerings. The Priors in office, Dante among them, had recourse to exceptional measures, banishing the leaders of the two factions: the Whites to Sarzana, the Blacks to Pieve del Toppo. But the banishment only caused bitterness and increased the tension in the city. An attempt at reconciliation, proposed by the Blacks at S. Trinità in 1301, came to nothing, with each party blaming the other for its failure. Finally Charles de Valois, brother of Philip IV of France, entered Florence on All Saints' Day as a mediator on behalf of Pope Boniface VIII, whom the Blacks looked to for support. Instead of mediating between the two parties, Charles turned the government over to the Blacks, inciting further partisan resentment and acts of revenge. Dante, on his way home from a diplomatic mission in Rome, was served notice of his sentence of banishment and death. He was never again to see his beloved native city.

In photo on left: The corner of the bridge of Ponte Vecchio where, according to tradition, Buondelmonte of the Buondelmonte clan was knifed to death by members of the Amidei and Uberti families for having reneged on his promised marriage with the daughter of Lambertuccio Uberti. This tragic murder took place on Easter of 1215.

DANTE ATTACKS THE "POLITICAL POPES"

Dante's attitude toward the papacy was complex. As a devout Christian he had a very lofty concept of the dignity of the Pope. He proclaimed that the authority of Scripture and the "Shepherd of the Church which guides you" should suffice for the salvation of Christians. When his enemy, Boniface VIII, was attacked and vulgarly insulted by the French in Anagni, Dante's Catholic conscience rose in defense of this affront to the Vicar of Christ. Nevertheless, he detested pontiffs who interfered in political matters, and he never forgot that he owed his exile from Florence to Boniface VIII and his supposed mediator, Charles de Valois. Boniface, the last of the warlike Popes of the Middle Ages, was as fixed and dogmatic in his ideas as Dante himself. Neither took into account the great political transformations afoot in Europe, the birth of national unity, the waning of the Holy Roman Empire. Boniface was a dogged exponent of the political supremacy of the papacy. In his view, society was identified with the Church, the Pope was its head, and the "two swords" of temporal and spiritual power belonged to him. If the king was granted the use of the temporal sword, it could be only *ad nutum Sacerdotis*, according to the directives of the High Priest. Dante savagely attacked such principles, insisting upon the distinction between the two powers and upon their autonomy in their respective spheres. The bitter attack on Rome which is one of the dominant themes of the *Divine Comedy* had its roots more in this ideological quarrel than in his indignation over corruption in Vatican circles. Boniface VIII is condemned to burn among the simoniacs in the place in Hell called Malebolge, literally evil pouches. A later pope, Clement V, is also consigned to Hell. For Dante, Clement was a "lawless shepherd," who never lost his loyalty to the King of his native France. The accusation of simony, or trafficking in spiritual offices, which the poet hurls at him was based in reality on a series of political moves: the transfer of the papal see to Avignon, and the support that he first gave and then withdrew from Henry VII, an unpardonable sin in Dante's eyes.

Below, left: Clement V as portrayed by Taddeo Gaddi in his fresco in Santa Maria Novella, in Florence. He was Bertrand de Got, archbishop of Bordeaux, and became Pope in 1305. His policy followed the directives of Philip the Fair. He was the first Pope to rule from Avignon instead of Rome. He also suppressed the Order of the Knights Templar. Below, right: A portrait of Boniface VIII, executed by Giotto and his assistants, in St. John Lateran. Boniface VIII proclaimed the Jubilee of 1300, in which Dante no doubt participated, since he recalls it in the Comedy. *Left: A page from the decretals of Boniface VIII.*

THE FINAL DISAPPOINTMENT

The Holy Roman Emperor Henry VII represented the last hope in Dante's political life. Everything depended on this Luxembourg prince who had reached the imperial throne through complicated political maneuvering behind the scenes. The first bitter taste of exile convinced Dante that there was no hope in his party's disorganized and impulsive attempt to make a comeback. The descent of the emperor into Italy in 1310 seemed to be an answer to his most ardent prayers. He was the savior who might punish the Blacks, return the exiles to Florence, and restore justice. A prisoner of his dream, Dante refused to see what a poor, pathetic man Henry was in reality. He refused, above all, to believe that the empire belonged to the past. When the emperor died, not on the field of battle, but in his bed of a fever, Dante's hopes were buried with him. But his faith remained: at the summit of Paradise, in the rose of the Blessed, an empty chair waits for Henry. It was the poet's supreme expression of loyalty.

Dante formulated his hopes for the coming of Henry VII to Italy in one of his Latin letters, which he dated "in the first year of the most fortunate coming of Caesar in Italy." In reality, there was nothing fortunate in the emperor's descent into Italy. In the summer of 1313, after arriving with his army at Bonconvento, near Siena, he died of malaria. Above, from left to right: Henry VII in Italy, at Cremona and probably at Asti, from a Codex in the Archives of Coblenz. On the adjoining page: His death, from a Codex in the Vatican Library.

enarono gran   to che piccolo apparecchiameto a

THE DIVINE COMEDY— A FOREST OF SYMBOLS

The Divine Comedy *has a distinct symbolic pattern throughout. From the moment in the "dark wood" when we come upon the three beasts that denote Dante's or mankind's spiritual bewilderment, the* Comedy *can be read allegorically, as the itinerary of mankind in search of blessedness. This profusion of symbols is in keeping with the medieval poet's role as educator and publicist. Dante uses fairly familiar symbols to make the abstract concepts of peace and justice, redemption and happiness, more accessible to the reader of his time. Parallel symbols help illuminate each other. Thus, the dark wood is contrasted with the Earthly Paradise, at the top of Mount Purgatory. Virgil personifies reason, which can lead man back to his lost earthly happiness; similarly, Beatrice personifies grace and theology, which raise man to divine happiness in the vision of God. Today's reader no longer responds to allegory, this long shadow of things which Dante projects on the world of the invisible. But many of the enigmas in the* Comedy *were clear to the 13th-century reader, who shared Dante's frame of reference. Left: The wild forest and the beasts, in an illustration by Zuccaro. Right, above: The same scene as imagined by Stradanus, a Flemish painter who settled in Florence in the 16th century. Below: The entrance to Hell, in a 19th-century print.*

"THE GENTLE FATHER"

The *Divine Comedy* makes clear Dante's affection for Virgil. He is the "gentle leader," the "courteous master," the "sage master," the "gentle father." Some see in Dante's choice of Virgil as his guide homage to the poet who glorified the Roman Empire; others recall that Virgil has first place among the excellent writers of antiquity cited as models in the *De Vulgari Eloquentia*. Nor must we forget that in the Middle Ages Virgil was considered a magician with a firsthand knowledge of the realm of the dead (Aeneas visits the Underworld in Virgil's *Aeneid*); medieval scholars saw in this pagan poet's work a prophecy of the coming of Christ, an interpretation which Dante subscribed to.

As regards Virgil's allegorical value in the poem, it is commonly held that he represents human reason. Perhaps those who view Virgil as a symbol of poetry, understood as art in general, are closer to the mark. But Dante's Virgil is more than the personification of an abstract idea. He is a mysterious and complex character. A grave melancholy, born of his awareness that he is excluded from Grace, is his habitual mood. In the realm of the dead, whether damned forever or awaiting salvation, Virgil is an outsider. His virtue is pagan virtue; as a pre-Christian soul, he can never see Paradise, but only the featureless calm of Limbo. This sorrow makes him silent. Compared to him, Dante is an extrovert: he shouts his enthusiasms and fears, utters doubts, recriminations and protests, and reveals himself freely. But Virgil remains closed within himself. His secret envelops him like a cloud.

There are many paintings of Virgil as Dante's teacher and guide. The painting (left) by Luca Signorelli, in the frescoes of the Chapel of San Brizio in the Cathedral of Orvieto, is suffused with the spirit of prophecy.

Above: Dante's Bark by Eugène Delacroix, showing Virgil next to Dante. This famous painting occasioned violent controversy among critics when it appeared in 1822. It marked a decisive turn in the art of that time; as the artist's first important work, it helped make Delacroix the standard-bearer of the Romantic movement in European painting. The painting is also a noteworthy document of the cult of Dante and his work which enjoyed a significant revival in the 19th century, after the neglect and denigration of the 17th and 18th centuries. This cult was first manifested in the arts, and then spread to the sphere of scholarly research and criticism throughout Europe.

A REALM OF SORROW

Dante is singularly economical with fire in his *Inferno*. No flames shoot up from the abyss plunging toward the center of the earth. Only four categories of sinners are punished by fire: the heretics, buried in fiery arcs; the violent against God, confined on dry, sandy soil on which flames rain slowly and continuously; the simoniacs, fixed in narrow holes, head downward, their soles licked at by flames; and the counselors of fraud, imprisoned within tongues of flame.

Eternal ice and cold torment the gluttons, whipped by hail and snow; those guilty of anger, caught in the mud in the Stygian marsh; the traitors, in the icy grip of Cocytus. Other torments are imaginative and horrible: the thick river of human blood in which homicides are immersed; the twisted, cursed trees in which the souls of suicides moan. Still others border on the grotesque.

But the worst torment of all, shared by every damned soul, is the consciousness of having lost God, a certainty that is confirmed by the inscription over the threshold of the "doleful city": "All hope abandon, ye who enter here." A heart-breaking nostalgia for earthly life is also vividly evoked: "the sweet air which rejoices in the sun," "the beautiful life, the happy time." This nostalgia exacerbates the pains of the damned. Master Adamo, the counterfeiter, for example, is condemned not only to eternal thirst but to the relentless memory of "the rivulets that from the verdant hills of Casentino descend into the Arno, making their channels cool and moist." The memory of what is irrevocably lost is the true meaning of Hell.

"HORNED DEMONS" AND "EVIL CLAWS"

If fire is scarce in Dante's *Inferno*, there is no shortage of devils: there are herds of them. They are typical medieval demons: horned, fanged and hairy, armed with whips or hooks. The first band of demons occupies the threshold of the City of Dis, numbering "more than a thousand"; a celestial messenger must disperse them so that Dante and his guide can pass. Another band of devils appears in the next *bolgia* (pouch), where lying seducers are punished: "horned demons with large scourges" who pitilessly belabor the backs of the damned, forcing them to run a breathless, endless race. But the worst demons are the *Malebranche*, literally Evil Claws, or by implication, the extensions or offspring of evil. They guard the barrators, those who trafficked in their public offices or authority for profit. Dante gives his imagination free rein among the *Malebranche*. Their names are highly expressive: Malacoda (Evil Tail), Alichino (Little Bent Wings), Calcabrina (Stepping On Salt), Barbariccia (Frizzy Beard), Cagnazzo (Bad Dog), Ciriatto (Curly), Graffiacane (Dog Scratcher), Farfarello (Butterfly), Libicocco (Lustful Dart), Rubicante (Ruddy), Scarmiglione (Scarlet). Their appearance conforms to the traditional iconography: they are all black; "a tusk like a hog's" protrudes from Ciriatto's mouth on either side; Farfarello grinds his teeth and rolls his eyes in his eagerness to strike the damned souls; all are armed with drag-hooks which tear off the flesh of their victims; all vent their ferocious glee with rude gestures and noises. Even more hideous is the isolated demon who dominates the chasm of the sowers of scandal and schism: he is at once a guard and an executioner, and wields a sword with which he viciously mutilates the damned passing by: we see Mosca de' Lamberti raising the stumps of his amputated hands, and Bertrand de Born swinging his severed head by the hair like a lantern. This cold horror paves the way for the encounter with three-headed Lucifer. "The Emperor of the Realm of Sorrow" is immersed up to his chest in the ice of the river Cocytus. The perpetual flapping of his bat-like wings raises an icy wind which freezes the Cocytus for eternity, while his three monstrous mouths tear and bite the three greatest sinners of antiquity according to Dante: Brutus and Cassius, the traitors of Caesar's Roman Empire, and Judas, the betrayer of God.

On these two pages, as on the two preceding ones, are some details from the cycle of frescoes executed by Luca Signorelli between 1499 and 1503 for the chapel of San Brizio in the Cathedral of Orvieto. The work was begun in 1447 by Beato Angelico, who limited himself to painting two arches of the vault. Luca Signorelli owes his fame to the frescoes inspired in part by the Divine Comedy. Although some of the individual figures stand out, the drama is above all entrusted to the mass, to that complicated tangle of bodies that occupies a great part of the composition. Even though it is overcrowded with figures— the tormented and the tormentors alike swept up in a common damnation—the composition reveals an order of its own which reflects that of the Comedy, of which the painter was an attentive and faithful interpreter.

Many underworld divinities of ancient mythology reappear in Dante's Inferno as monsters or demons. Whatever dignity they had has disappeared in order to give place to horror. Minos, who according to the Greeks was one of the judges in the tribunal of Hades, has become a mere executor of divine justice, which he administers in a bestial way bordering on the grotesque. Similarly Pluto, the ancient god of riches degraded to the status of a demon, is addressed by Virgil as a cursed wolf. The first illustrators of the Divine Comedy indulged their fantasy with these and other sinister figures, as is confirmed by these pictures taken from Codex 2253 of the Trivulziana Library in Milan. From left to right they represent: Pluto and Minos, and (below) Lucifer and the Harpies.

ON THE LEDGES OF PURGATORY

Dante and Virgil, after reaching the center of the globe where Lucifer is fixed in ice, leave the Inferno behind them. Crossing the hidden road that leads them to the banks of Purgatory, they begin to mount upward *"again to see the stars."* As we can see from the fresco by Domenico di Michelino in Santa Maria del Fiore (left), Purgatory is like an immense mountain rising from the waters which, according to the ancients, occupied the whole Southern Hemisphere. The mount of expiation is an inverted cone, at the summit of which is the "divine forest thick and alive" of the Earthly Paradise. Seven ledges encircle the mountain. One of the mortal sins is punished on each one of them. Souls must remain there for a period of time consonant with the gravity of their sin. Dante himself, taking a quick look at his conscience, says that he foresees that he will not remain for long among the envious, whereas his stay on the ledge of the proud will be exceedingly long. But not all souls have quick access to the mount of expiation. At the foot of the mountain, near the shore where the two travelers land in the bark of an angel-boatman, there is a kind of a quarantine camp for those who repented only in the last moments of their lives. The excommunicated who died repentant, but in contumacy of Holy Church, are gathered in a group to one side. Such souls must wait even longer before they can begin the slow and tortuous climb up the ledges of the mountain.

45

WHERE PAIN IS HOPE

The change of setting and atmosphere in the passage from the *Inferno* to the *Purgatorio* gives the measure of a changed spiritual climate. The gloom and darkness of the realm of sorrow is followed by the crystalline purity of a dawn over the sea, the stench of the foul air of Hell by a marine saltiness and the fragrance of dew-covered grass, the infernal shouts, screams and curses by the murmur of sea and wind, and immediately afterward a song of liberation. The landscape of Purgatory is typically Italian; indeed at the landing-place it is Tuscan: a shore bathed by placid waters with a mountainous backdrop behind them. The very ledges of the mount of expiation are reminiscent of parts of the Umbrian Appenines, which look like vast staircases. This landscape culminates in the forest of the Earthly Paradise, a sublimated image of the pine forest of Ravenna, one of the poet's favorite places. It has been said that the *Purgatorio* is the most exquisitely pictorial of the canticles, but it is also suffused with sound. At times a single line of verse—"There, seated on the grass and on the flowers, singing *Salve Regina* saw I souls"—suffices to create an unforgettable musical frame and setting. Feelings are attuned to the sweetness of the landscape: the most cruel memories have lost their harshness, even the polemical note is muted. The most constant theme is that of spiritual solidarity, which binds together the souls and even the loved ones left behind on earth. There is a vast current of love linking the quick and the dead. It is thanks to love that Forese Donati, who died only five years before Dante's poetic journey, is almost at the top of the mountain, close to liberation. He has been brought so far by the prayers of his good wife, Nella, whom he so neglected in his earthly life. This also explains the penitents who plead with Dante to tell their loved ones to pray for them. Purgatory is a place of expiation, but also one of correction. The very pains of the souls there are sweet, because they are mingled with hope.

46

The Frenchman Gustave Doré was one of the most famous and successful illustrators of the Divine Comedy. He executed the three scenes on this page relating to the Purgatorio.
Left: The encounter with Forese Donati, who will point out some companions to Dante. One of them is Bonagiunta da Lucca, with whom the poet will talk about the "sweet New Style."
Above: The proud who occupy the first of the ledges of the Purgatorio and (right) a group of gluttons. The souls in purgatory are punished differently than the damned. For example, the misers are stretched out on the ground to symbolize their attachment to earthly things. The lecherous are driven by a whirlwind like the damned, but they walk among the purifying flames of their ledge. Here Dante obviously recalls the ardor of amorous passion.

THREE
BLESSED LADIES

Three Blessed Ladies help start Dante on his journey. Virgil tells him about them in the "dark wood," when Dante becomes so frightened he wants to drop the whole project then and there. The first is Mary, although Virgil does not speak her name, just as he does not mention the name of Christ during the whole tour of Hell. Those names would be contaminated if pronounced in the realm of sin. Mary is the "gentle lady," who represents Divine Grace. Taking pity on Dante, she entrusts him to Lucia, the virgin martyr of Syracuse, who is the traditional patroness of those with weak sight, and stands for Illuminating Grace. Lucia, in turn, obtains the intervention of Beatrice, who persuades Virgil to act as Dante's guide. The colloquy between the pagan poet and the "lady of virtue" is right out of the romances of chivalry. Beatrice pleads and coaxes, her eyes bright with tears. Virgil, an excellent knight, promises to do her bidding promptly. During the hardest parts of the journey, Virgil evokes the image of Beatrice to animate his companion: "I know not if thou understand, I speak of Beatrice, thou shalt see her abode, on the summit of this mount, smiling and blessed."

Later, more Blessed Ladies greet the poet. The first is Matilda, the genius of Eden, who goes along "singing and culling flower after flower" in the Earthly Paradise. In the course of the mystic procession three most noble ladies advance, dressed in white, red and green, followed by four others dressed in purple. They are easily recognizable as the theological and cardinal virtues. As in the encounter between Beatrice and Virgil, the scene suggests a reflection of ancient memories.

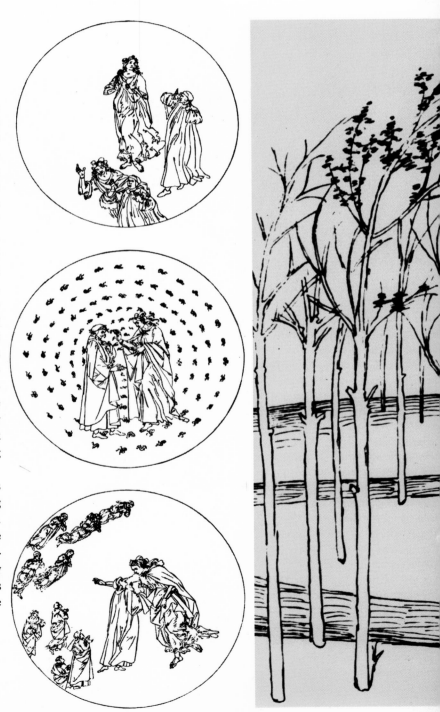

Below: From Sandro Botticelli's illustrations for the Divine Comedy, *the instant at which Dante and Beatrice rise from the forest of the Earthly Paradise, atop the Mount of Purgatory where they have met after ten years, and fly toward heaven. In the circles on the adjoining page (left): Botticelli's visions of Paradise. Bottom: Beatrice points out the various Blessed to Dante; middle: the poet and his lady in the heaven of Venus, among the loving souls who look like flames; finally, top: Dante and Beatrice, caught in two different poses by the painter, in the heights of the heaven of Jove where the spirits of the just triumph. The whole* Paradiso *is a glorification of Beatrice, who becomes ever more splendid and beautiful as the pilgrims draw closer and closer to God. She is for the poet a mother, teacher and guide: she resolves the doubts that plague him, and defines deep questions of theology and morality, typical of the third canticle.*

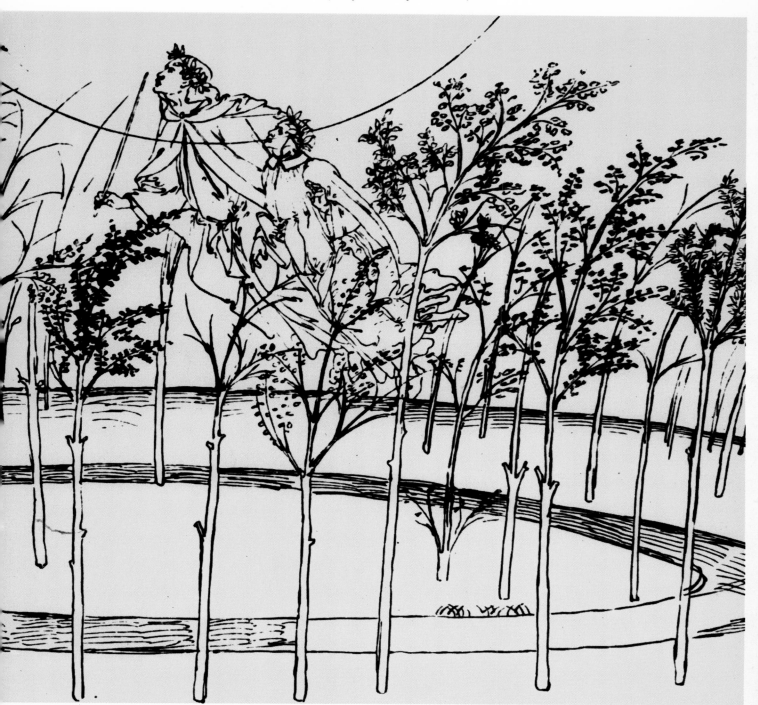

THE DAZZLING DIVINE VISION

On this and adjoining page: Details from the series painted in 1400 by Friar John of Fiesole, known as Beato Angelico. It is preserved today in St. Mark's Monastery in Florence. The visions of Paradise shown here complement Dante's imagination. Their exceptional simplicity, clarity of form and fine use of color are typical of Angelico's paintings, which magnify the glory of the Beati, or Blessed, and their otherworldly happiness.

Dante's Paradise is all sound and light: contours are lost, lines fade, images vanish in an ocean of brightness which becomes more and more luminous until it is barely tolerable to the human eye. Unlike Hell and Purgatory, Heaven bears no resemblance to Italy or any other earthly landscape. Everything melts in a vast stream of light from which an ineffable harmony is released. Even the features of the Blessed disappear in dazzling light. The Blessed, variously represented as images in a mirror, fish in a pond, and lamps or sparks shimmering against a background of brightness, do not stand out in individual relief like the damned, ever isolated and alone in their torment. We see them rather in the mass, a community animated by mutual love. The configurations in which the Blessed shine forth and dance—circles in the heaven of the Sun, glittering cross in Mars, lily and eagle in Jove, shining ladder in Saturn—are images of the love they bear toward each other and in God.

Dante's spectacular images of light are a remarkable feat of imagination for a man of the 13th century. No electricity, neon or fireworks existed then. Only pallid lanterns in houses, candles on altars, and bonfires in the country broke the darkness of the medieval night. The stream of light that spreads from heaven to heaven, at last blazing forth in the "white rose" of the Blessed, is a miracle of the poet's vision.

THE WORLD IS NOT FORGOTTEN

Below: The Madonna appearing to St. Bernard, by the Rinuccini Chapel Master. The last canto of the Paradiso opens with St. Bernard's invocation to the Virgin, asking that Dante may be given the strength to bear the supreme vision of God and His mysteries.

Dazzling as Heaven is, the world is not forgotten in the *Paradiso*. It is the work of a man who senses the approach of death. After years of bitterness and disappointment, his soul turns to heaven. The earth appears tiny, as though seen from an immense distance. Yet even in the loftiness of the heavens the poet reveals his humanity. He expresses the hope that he will be able to return to Florence and to the beautiful church of San Giovanni, not on the wave of political events, but by virtue of his poem, whose merits will fling open the gates of his native city. This supreme and moving hope is destined, like the others, to remain unfulfilled.

The saintly founders of the religious orders have words of comfort for Dante, and indignation for the corruption of their followers. The harshest invective in the entire *Comedy* is St. Peter's tirade on the decadence of the Roman Curia. Finally it is St. Bernard, the devout servant of the Blessed Virgin, who with his prayer to the Queen of Heaven obtains for Dante a unique privilege for a mortal: the brief, blinding vision of the glory of God.

Left: One of Giotto's frescoes in the St. Francis of Assisi cycle on the saint's life. Here, Pope Innocent III dreams of St. Francis supporting the Church. Canto XI of the Paradiso *tells how the saint "royally his stern intent to Innocent revealed, and from him had the first imprint upon his Order."*

CRITICISM
AND CURSES

Despite the universality of the *Divine Comedy*, with
its great theme of man's search for salvation, the poem
can be read on one level as an impassioned, partisan
discourse on Italian politics in the 13th century. All of
Dante's bitterness and indignation come out in his
poetry. As many of the souls he meets on his journey
are local figures, he finds numerous occasions to curse
his enemies. This is especially true in the *Inferno*. Proud
Florence and her ungrateful people, he hopes, will soon
be punished by hostile neighbors. Pistoia is so filled
with evil and corruption that the whole city would be
better burned to the ground. To destroy Pisa, he calls
upon the islands of Capraia and Gorgona to block the
mouth of the Arno, making the river overflow and
drown the entire Pisan population. Even in the *Purgatorio*, there is a diatribe against Italy. Loving his country, Dante is outraged by its endless strife and its
rebelliousness against imperial authority. But as he
continues his journey, as the atmosphere becomes more
spiritual and the poet's soul more pure, his fury dies
down; he becomes resigned to waiting for justice.

Another great object of criticism is the Church,
which Dante accuses of corruption and worldliness.
The greed for material goods which contaminates so
many of the clergy is a recurring theme. In the *Paradiso*, he puts his accusations in the mouths of the
Blessed, whose purity is itself a criticism of the faulty
men on earth. In the lower heavens, they cry out
against the impiety of ordinary Christians; later they
turn to corruption in the Church itself. Religious orders
have become lax; convents have been invaded by
worldly desires; scheming prelates devote themselves
to acquiring wealth and power. The climax of all this
invective is St. Peter's censure of Dante's enemy, Pope
Boniface VIII.

Below: The Donation of Constantine to Pope Liberius in a painting by Raffaello del Colle (Vatican). This act, sanctioned by a document which the humanist Lorenzo Valla proved to be a forgery, was considered historically authentic during the Middle Ages. Dante too believed it was genuine and cursed the donation of Constantine as the origin of temporal power. Left: Meeting of the Mantuan Virgil and his compatriot Sordello, by Goito, in a 19th-century woodcut. The episode is the theme of Canto VI of the Purgatorio; it offered Dante, by contrast, an argument against the discords prevailing in Italy. The poet also deplores the activity of ecclesiastics who impede the pacifying mission of the Empire.

PAOLO AND FRANCESCA

Paolo Malatesta and Francesca da Rimini are the best known and most pitied of all of Dante's damned souls. The poet is moved to the point of fainting when Francesca tells her story.

The tale is as simple as it is tragic. Francesca was the wife of Gianciotto Malatesta, Paolo's older brother. One day while reading the French romance *Lancelot du Lac* together, the two young people fell in love. Betrayed by a third brother, the lovers were surprised and killed by the angry husband. In Hell, they are condemned to be swept along perpetually in the "infernal storm."

Dante's pity for these "wearied souls" must have arisen from a sense of involvement. As a boy of 17 or 18 he knew Paolo Malatesta, who was Captain of the Commune in Florence in 1282 and 1283. Francesca's brother, Bernardino da Polenta, was his companion-in-arms at the battle of Campaldino, after the lovers' death. He had read the popular romance that provoked their passion.

Although Gianciotto's act was a "crime of honor," justified and even praised by some commentators, it is the ill-starred couple, defiantly and hopelessly in love even after death, who arouse our compassion and Dante's.

Ever since Dante popularized it, the tragedy of Francesca da Rimini and Paolo Malatesta has inspired artists in every field: Poetry, drama, music and painting. The theme of the unfortunate lovers appealed to many painters in the Romantic period. On the adjoining page (left) are two famous paintings, the first executed by the German Anselm Feuerbach, who died in Venice in 1880, and the second (below) by Ary Scheffer, who is considered the chief Romantic painter of Holland. On this page: A 14th-century miniature on the subject; and (below) a romantic and colorful interpretation by Amos Cassioli.

TWO WOMEN: VICTIM AND PARTISAN

Dante meets only two women in Purgatory. Pia de' Tolomei was the pathetic victim of a 13th-century "divorce Italian style": she was killed in a remote castle in Maremma by the order of her husband, who wanted to plunge into another marriage. Pia tells her story without a word of accusation; like a deer shot by hunters, she is filled with a mild wonder. Her heartbreaking defenselessness has made her a perennial object of readers' sympathy.

Sapia, the second woman, is less pitiable but far more vivid. The wife of Ghinibaldo Saracini, a Sienese lord, and the aunt of Provenzano Salvani, the proud Ghibelline leader who humbled himself to beg for the ransom of a friend, Sapia is a woman of a single passion: envy. For Dante this term still had its Latin connotation of hatred. Sapia detested her Ghibelline compatriots with a fanatic violence: as long as she could see them ruined, she was willing to be swept up in the destruction herself. When she relives her exultation upon seeing the Sienese routed at the battle of Colle, the verse vibrates with the echo of a savage laughter. More than one thousand of her fellow citizens died in that battle, and another 1,500 were taken prisoner by the French and Florentine forces.

The 19th-century commentators disapproved of this violent woman. But Sapia the partisan found grace in the eyes of Dante, himself a man of partisan passions. When "on the brink of my life" Sapia turned to God, she must have done so with the same passionate intensity with which she had known how to hate. Great sinners make great converts.

Pia, the penitent whom Dante meets in Canto V of the Purgatorio, *was, according to early commentators, the wife of a certain Nello dei Pannocchieschi da Petra di Siena. Lord of a castle in Maremma, he is presumed to have died in 1322, one year after Dante.*

Left: Dante's encounter with Pia in a woodcut by Gustave Doré. Above: The palace of the Tolomei in Siena and, on right, Sapia's house in two drawings by Viligiardi. The victory which so gladdened Sapia took place at Colle in 1269.

TWO LADIES OF PARADISE

Below: Piccarda in an illustration by C. Laurenti. Next to her in the heaven of the Moon is another famous nun forcibly removed from a convent: Constance d'Altavilla, a Norman princess. She was the bride of Henry VI of Swabia and the mother of Frederick II. On adjoining page: Sordello and Cunizza in the 19th-century painting by Faruffini. A sister of the tyrant of Padua, Ezzelino da Romano, Cunizza was the protectress and friend of the troubador of Goito, whom Dante placed among the negligent sinners in the small flower-strewn valley of the Anti-Purgatorio. The lunette above the painting connects this episode with the encounter with Cunizza in the Paradiso.

There are more ladies in Paradise than in Purgatory. A woman is the first to step forward in the milky brightness of the heaven of the Moon. She is Piccarda Donati. The poet's memory is stirred because Piccarda was the sister of Forese, Corso and Sinibaldo, the "Disreputables" of Florence during Dante's youth; she was also the cousin of Dante's wife, Gemma. Piccarda had not succumbed to the raging thirst for power and pleasure which drove the men of her family; she sought only the love of God. But she was also swept up in the madness of the Donati family; Corso's henchmen came to drag her forcibly away from the convent she had chosen in order to marry her to a political ally of the moment, Rossellino della Tosa. She soon died: some said of a mysterious leprosy, others, of sorrow. Dante found her "in the sphere that moveth slowest," among the souls of those prevented by force from fulfilling their religious vows.

Not far from Piccarda is Cunizza da Comano. She is the last woman one would expect to find in Paradise because, according to an ancient commentator, "she was enamoured at every age, and was so bountiful with her love that she would have deemed it an act of rudeness to deny it to anyone who had courteously asked for it." She had had three husbands and an undetermined number of lovers. Cunizza's appearance in the heaven of Venus has produced rivers of ink from the pens of critics. Why was Dante so generous to a woman with such a checkered background? It may have been because the young Dante knew Cunizza as an old woman; he met her in the Cavalcanti house, where she had found refuge after being expelled from her lands. She too, therefore, had eaten the bitter bread of exile. Perhaps it was this that made her sacred in his eyes.

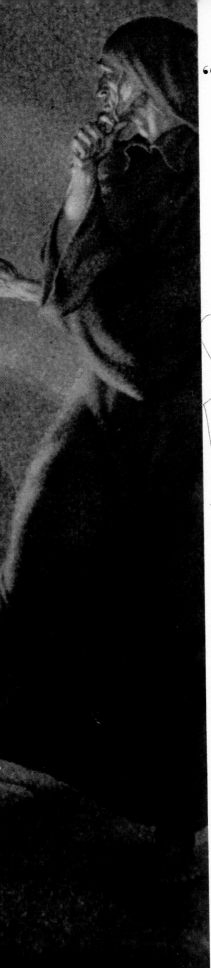

"I ALONE DEFENDED HER"

Farinata degli Uberti, born around 1200, was a man of great culture and courage. An expert in military matters, he took part in the bloody battle of Montaperti. He died in 1264. Almost 20 years after his death, in 1283, he was condemned as a heretic by an inquisitor who had his remains and those of his wife removed from consecrated ground.

Another renowned inhabitant of the *Inferno* is Farinata degli Uberti, head of the Ghibelline party in Florence for more than 25 years. The fame of the passage rests upon a single line: "I alone defended her (Florence) with open face." This statement became a political slogan in later Italian history.

But the encounter has a deeper importance. It demonstrates the force of the passions politics aroused in 13th-century Italy. As Dante, a Guelph and a descendant of Guelphs, and his opponents' leader debate, they are swept away. The rapid and driving character of the exchange makes it one of the most theatrical passages in the entire poem. Virgil stands silent and ignored. Hell itself is forgotten; nothing matters to the disputants but their irreconcilable arguments.

The debate is reaching its climax when it is interrupted by a tragic apparition: the shade of Cavalcante de' Cavalcanti, father of Guido, Dante's closest friend. Dante parries the wretched man's questions about his son, who is already suffering from the malaria that will kill him that same year. Cavalcante is alarmed: "Lives he not still? Does not the sweet light strike his eyes?" When Dante continues to hesitate, he falls back into the flames, overcome with anguish.

This pathetic incident underlines Farinata's single-mindedness. Cavalcante's misery would move the most hardened; and Guido's fate surely should affect Farinata, who happened to be his son-in-law. But Farinata is unmoved. As soon as Cavalcante stops talking, he picks up the thread of his own speech exactly where it was interrupted, talking determinedly on about his faction and the battle of Montaperti. He stands for all time as the prototype of the politician, who cares for nothing that does not concern his party.

Left: The episode of Farinata as interpreted by Amos Nattini, one of the most noted Italian illustrators of the Comedy. *Above: The Ghibelline chief in a portrait by Andrea del Castagno, preserved today in the Cenacolo di Sant'Apollonia in Florence.*

THE TRAGEDY OF UGOLINO

One of the unhappiest souls in Hell is Count Ugolino of Pisa. Dante comes upon him gnawing at the skull of his archenemy Archbishop Ruggieri, and he tells his story on a crescendo of horror. The count, separated from his troops after a disastrous battle, was shipwrecked; when he returned to Pisa, he was accused of treason. With his children, he was walled up in the Tower of Hunger. Ugolino describes the reverberation of the hammers in the dawn; he tells how his smallest son asks what is wrong with his father, being too young to realize that his own coffin is being sealed. Panic is succeeded by despair. Finally, "hunger overcame sorrow." This controversial line has been taken by some to mean that Ugolino added the supreme horror of cannibalism to his misfortunes. In any event, the final image is that of the father groping in the dark among his children's corpses.

This tragic story comes out of the gloomiest medieval chronicles. Its historical reality adds nothing to its poetic truth. The real Ugolino was a chronic political traitor. He betrayed everybody: the Ghibellines, the Guelphs and even his own nephew. In addition, the youths who were incarcerated with him were not as young as Dante portrays them: two were Ugolino's adult sons, the others his grandsons. But Dante cared little about their real identity. On their images he superimposed others: those of his own sons, left alone and undefended in the city from which he was banished. When Ugolino says, "I heard my sons who were with me, weeping in their sleep," and when his son cries, "My father! Why don't you help me?"—their despair springs from the poet's nightmare of exile. These were the voices that Dante himself heard in the long nights.

PITY FOR
MANFRED, GLORY
FOR CACCIAGUIDA

"King Manfred," says the historian Villani, "was as handsome as his father and even more dissolute. He was a musician and singer. He liked to see jugglers, courtiers and lovely women around him, and always dressed in green. He was very generous, courteous and even-tempered, so that he was much loved. But all his life he was an Epicurean, almost never concerning himself with God or the saints. . . ." Manfred, a natural son of Frederick II, shone like an evening star in the twilight of the Ghibelline Empire. Like many other profligates, he fell valiantly in battle. But unlike most of them, he died repentant, at peace with God. Dante uses him to glorify divine mercy. Perhaps he himself had some partiality for the personage. God's forgiveness is in sharp contrast with human mercilessness: Manfred was refused burial because he had been excommunicated. There is a brief but unforgettable allusion to the removal of his remains "with tapers quenched," and their abandonment to the inclemency of wind and rain. Through Manfred, Dante seems to be asking pity for all the dead against whom the hatred of men rages.

Cacciaguida, the crusader whom Dante meets in the high heaven of Mars, acts as a foil for Manfred, the less perfect hero. Cacciaguida was the poet's great-great-grandfather. His colloquy with Dante occupies three whole cantos, and yet he reveals much less of his character than does Manfred in 40 lines. His virtue deprives him of personality. His exemplary death in the war against the infidels and his place among the Blessed are arguments for the poet's intended thesis to express the growing decadence of Florence, compared to earlier times, in which a greater justice and dignity prevailed. This illustrious ancestor also predicted Dante's exile, which began in 1302, two years after his poetic "journey."

Left: Manfred, King of Sicily, at the battle of Benevento in an illustration by Magrini. Handsome and knightly, a patron of scholars and poets, Manfred was overcome by the forces that allied themselves against his ambitious dream. As Dante reminds us, it was the Archbishop of Cosenza who ordered that his remains be removed and cast to the elements.

Giovanni Fattori, a Tuscan painter noted for his military themes, imagined Cacciaguida fighting against the infidels as shown in the above painting. Dante's great-great-grandfather actually died in the Holy Land. His historical existence is proved by a document of 1189. He was a crusader in the army of Conrad III of Swabia, whom Dante confused with Conrad the Salic.

VERONA REMINDS HIM OF HIS LOST FLORENCE

The city of Verona was "the first refuge and the first abode" that Dante found after his condemnation and banishment in 1302. He arrived there in 1303, or at the latest in 1304, still aching from the pain of exile. The city had a vague similarity to Florence, comforting to the unhappy poet. Like Florence, Verona nestled among smiling hills, and had a river spanned by sturdy bridges. The walls that enclosed it were new; but the old Roman town could still be traced in the geometric distribution of the streets and quarters. The battlements of Ghibelline palaces rose above the hovels of the common people. The communal democracy, briefly restored after the fall of the tyrant Ezzelino da Romano, was now definitively in decline: the government was in the hands of the first signory of the new era. Its leader was Scaligeri, who after being elected Captain of the People managed to make it a lifetime job. This system was to be followed, with few variations, by almost all of the founders of the signory. Dante lived in Verona twice, before and after Henry VII's descent into Italy. Each time his stay there stretched over a period of years, proof that Dante had found a friendly and congenial atmosphere.

Dante found space in the *Comedy* to praise his friend and host in Verona, Cangrande della Scala. Their friendship was based on identical political views. The city had been traditionally for the Empire, and at that time Cangrande was a recognized leader among the Ghibellines. He was less sympathetic to his guest's art than to his politics. The anecdotes about Cangrande that survive indicate that in his eyes the prestige of a man of letters hardly equaled that of a good falconer.

Left: The monument to Dante in Verona, in front of the ancient palace of the Scaligeri, was executed by Ugo Zanoni. This is one of the few monuments dedicated to Italy's greatest poet. Many years ago the Italian Parliament voted to erect a national monument to him in Rome, but the project never materialized.

Above, from top to bottom: Dante with Uguccione della Faggiuola at the court of Cangrande, in a 19th-century print. The question of the friendship between Dante and Uguccione is still disputed. Bottom: The equestrian statue of Cangrande della Scala in Rome.

NO PEACE FOR THE EXILE

Places where Dante stayed during his wanderings. Left: A medieval palace in Lucca. Right: The castle of Fosdinovo, and (below), the fortress of Castelnuovo, both the property of the Malaspina family. Large landowners in Lunigiana, this family offered generous hospitality to the poet; he served them as ambassador and diplomat on various confidential missions.

Dante remained a wanderer throughout the 19 years of his exile, which lasted from 1302 until his death. He was not the kind of man to find a second homeland. He moved from city to city, from court to court, always hoping for a reversal of fortune which would reopen the gates of ungrateful Florence to him. Those were hard times for exiles. Italy was teeming with politicians in disgrace; neither Dante's nobility nor his art represented a passport to special privilege. The figure of the courtier-artist, which was to be so familiar in the great courts of the Renaissance, was not yet known in Dante's time. Rulers' patronage of the arts, with its pensions for poets, was still a thing of the future. In any case, Dante would have never bent the knee to play such a role. The potentates who gave him asylum were typical warlords: rough, ignorant and arrogant. Save for the Malaspina, whose hospitality was noted in troubadour poetry, they had but a lukewarm interest in art. A poet was an entertainer, like a clown—certainly not a genius. That Dante was a man of culture meant only that he could carry out secretarial duties and diplomatic missions; he was also useful as a propagandist for the pro-imperial party, for which he wrote a kind of manifesto, the *De Monarchia*.

It is ironic that the warlords were much impressed by Dante's reputation as a sorcerer, an expert on the realms beyond the grave. For the moment this popular legend was the poet's only reward for his great *Comedy*. One of the Viscontis of Milan, in order to persuade a priest noted for his sorcery to perform certain evil rites for him, threatened to hire Dante Alighieri instead. The purpose of the evil spell was to hasten the death of Pope John XXII with opportune "charms." The specter of competition induced the priest to agree. But then he rushed to the pontifical court and confessed this abuse of his office.

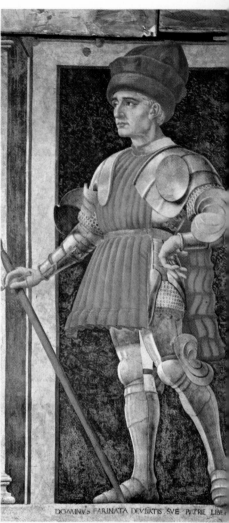

DOMINVS FARINATA DEVERTIS SVE PATRIE LIBER

Left: The castle of Romena in the Casentino, one of the residences of the Counts Guidi, supporters of the Ghibelline party; Dante was a guest there. Below it: The Benedictine abbey of Pomposa, about 30 miles from Ravenna, where the poet stayed on his return journey from Venice in the summer of 1321. He was already suffering from the fever that would cause his death.

In the painting (below) by Bertini, Dante hands the manuscript of the Inferno to Fra Ilario. According to a widespread but unverified legend, the poet is supposed to have arrived at a monastery at the mouth of the Magra, as an unknown pilgrim en route to France. The monk took the manuscript from him for ultimate delivery to Uguccione della Faggiuola.

RAVENNA—THE LAST HAVEN

The pine wood of Ravenna, which offered Dante a quiet asylum for his meditations in the latter part of his life. The poet took up residence here. He was soon joined by his sons Pietro and Jacopo, and a daughter, Antonia, who after his death entered a convent under the name of Sister Beatrice. The Paradiso was certainly composed during his stay in Ravenna; he finished it almost on the eve of his death. In fact, after his death, his family doubted that the final cantos had been written. The poet's ghost appeared in a dream to his son Jacopo, pointing out to him their secret hiding place.

On adjoining page, above: The Church of St. Francis in Ravenna, site of Dante's first burial. Later the Florentines, supported by the Medici Pope Leo X, claimed his remains. The friars then hid his bones, and when the tomb was opened it was empty. In 1865, during restoration work, the coffer containing the poet's remains was found in a niche hollowed out in the wall of the Braccioforte chapel. The coffer was then placed in a marble vault. Below: The painting by Mochi shows Dante presenting his friend Giotto to Guido Novello da Polenta, lord of Ravenna, who gave the painter a worthy welcome.

Ravenna was the last place where Dante found peace and quiet. If Verona had been his first refuge amid the raging storms, Ravenna was the safe harbor, in which Dante gathered in his sails. When he arrived, he was still sustained by the thought that the *Comedy* might fling open again the gates of the "beautiful sheepfold." He had expressed this hope at the end of his journey into the world beyond, at the summit of Paradise.

The earthly pilgrimage was also coming to an end. Dante was a little more than 50 now, older in suffering than in years. He describes himself as emaciated and broken, with a bent back. He was now in a hurry to complete the *Comedy*, as though he sensed that his days were numbered. He sent the *Paradiso* to Cangrande with a dedicatory letter, even though it still lacked 13 cantos. The latter were composed so rapidly that his family, at his death, did not yet know they existed.

Ravenna was a fine place for meditation. It was a small city, ruled by a wise, moderate lord who loved study: Guido Novello da Polenta, a nephew of Francesca da Rimini. The atmosphere was attuned to the melancholy of the poet. And Ravenna had a pine wood, like the "thick and luxuriant divine forest" of the Earthly Paradise, the haven for purified souls at the summit of the Mount of Purgatory. The journey of expiation was now over for Dante too. The friendly shades of the forest and the murmur of the pines welcomed him for the last time on his return from a diplomatic mission to Venice, in the late summer of 1321. The poet was trembling with fever. His weakened constitution offered no resistance to an attack of malaria. He died on the night of September 13, surrounded by his children and friends. Guido Novello da Polenta laid a laurel wreath on his cold forehead.

Left: The Death of Dante, *detail of a painting by Anselm Feuerbach. Born in Spira in 1829, this German painter studied, among other places, in Munich. He also worked in Paris, where he was a pupil of Couture. Many of his paintings illustrate themes from the* Divine Comedy, *and are enveloped* in an atmosphere of passionate Romanticism. *Below:* Blessed Dante *by Nardo di Cione, in the Church of Santa Maria Novella in Florence. Heaven and Hell are faithfully depicted as Dante described them. The artist portrayed Dante himself among the Blessed, in a contemplative attitude.*

1265—May: born in Florence, son of Alighiero II, son of Bellincione.

1274—at the age of nine he sees Beatrice, daughter of Folco Portinari, for the first time.

1275—begins his studies at the convents of Santa Croce and Santa Maria Novella.

1277—February 9: is formally betrothed to Gemma Donati.

1282—completes his studies.

1283—writes his first sonnets.

1285—November 30: he becomes a soldier and takes part in the battle of the Sienese against the Aretines at Poggio Santa Cecilia.

1287—probably goes to Bologna.

1288—writes the song "Ladies who have intelligence of love" and the two sonnets "Love is one with the gentle heart" and "My lady bears love in her eyes."

1289—June 11: takes part in the Battle of Campaldino, between the Guelph forces and the Ghibellines under the command of Vieri de' Cerchi. August 16: he participates in the siege of the fortress of Caprona conducted by the Lucchesi against the Pisans.

1290—June 8: Beatrice dies.

1292–1293—the years of waywardness. Toward the end of this period he probably begins his married life with Gemma Donati, who will bear him two boys and two girls.

1294—he establishes a friendship with Carlo Martello, son of Charles d'Anjou.

1295—July 6: he enrolls in the Guild of Doctors and Druggists and enters Florentine political life. December: he is elected to the council of the Heads of the Arts in order to cooperate with the Captain of the People in the selection of new Priors.

1296—June 15: he takes part in the Council of the Hundred.

1300—May Day: beginning of the factional struggles between the Cerchi and the Donati. May 7: he is sent as ambassador to San Gimignano to persuade the commune to join the Guelph party. June 15–August 14: he is named a Prior.

1301—June 29: he takes the floor in the Council of the Hundred to oppose helping Boniface VIII fight the Santafiora of Maremma. October: he is sent to Rome as an ambassador to Boniface VIII to convince him to recall Charles de Valois, whom the Pope has sent to Florence as a mediator. November: Corso Donati re-enters Florence and wreaks vengeance on the Whites.

1302—January 27: accused of barratry; in Siena, he receives news of his sentence: a fine of 5,000 small florins and banishment for two years with permanent exclusion from public office. March 10: for failure to appear in court, he is condemned to death in absentia.

1303—at Forli as assistant and secretary to Scarpetta Ordelaffi. October 12: Boniface VIII dies.

1304—July 20: new defeat of the Whites near the fortress of Lastra a Signa. Dante arrives in Verona, welcomed by Alboino della Scala.

1305—probably starts writing the treatises "Convivio" and "De Vulgari Eloquentia."

1306—October 6: moves to Lunigiana, and is appointed procurator to the Marquesses Malaspina. The beginnings of the "Comedy" probably date from this period.

1310—at the news of the arrival in Italy of Henry VII of Luxembourg, he goes to meet his fellow exiles at Forli. October: with other exiles, he goes to Asti to pay homage to Henry VII.

1311—January 6: Henry VII is crowned King of Italy in Milan. April 16: Dante writes a letter to the emperor inviting him to come into Tuscany and restore peace to Florence.

1312—March-April: joins Henry VII in Pisa. June 29: Henry VII is crowned in Rome at St. John Lateran. Rome is occupied by the militia of Robert d'Anjou, king of Naples; Pope Clement V, from Avignon, orders Henry to leave the city, but the emperor refuses. September 19: the emperor camps under the walls of Florence.

1313—August 24: the emperor moves from Pisa toward the Kingdom of Naples. He dies of fever during the journey.

1314—April 20: Clement V dies. September 7: the poet is the guest of Cangrande della Scala in Verona.

1315—the signory grants an amnesty to the exiles, but Dante refuses to return to Florence under the conditions imposed. October: he leaves Verona for Lucca. November 6: a new Florentine sentence confirms the sentence against the exiles and extends it to their families.

1316–1319—travels between Verona, the Marca Trevigiana, Romagna, and Tuscany. In 1318 he is in Ravenna as the guest of Guido Novello da Polenta.

1321—August: ambassador to Venice, on a mission for Guido Novello, he is stricken with fever and returns to Ravenna. September: dies on the night of the 13th. Guido buries him in the Church of St. Francis with full honors.